FEMINISM AND TECHNOLOGY WOR(L)DS

Freerange Vol. 10

Published by Freerange Press
Aotearoa, Atlantis, Australia

Editor
Jessie Moss

Editorial advisor
Emma Johnson

Design
Maia McDonald

Freerange wishes to thank all those who have provided support, assistance or contributions during the creative process. Also available as a download on our website:
www.projectfreerange.com

Published July 2015
ISBN 9780473327989 (print)
ISBN 9780473327996 (online)
ISSN 1179-8106 (print)
ISSN 1179-8114 (online)

Freerange Vol.10 by Freerange Cooperative is licensed under a Creative Commons Attribution Non-Commercial No Derivatives Licence. This licence allows users to share the journal or articles for non-commercial purposes, so long as the article is reproduced in the whole without changes, and the original authorship is acknowledged. This does not mean that you can ignore the original copyright of the contributors in their work as the author's moral rights are in no way affected by these licence terms.

For more information on these rights please go to this address: www.creativecommons.org or contact us for details.

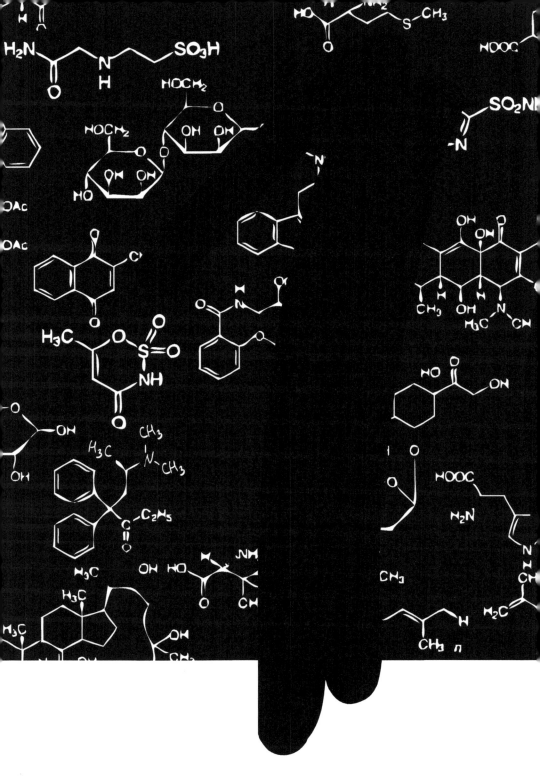

Feminism has fought no wars. It has killed no opponents. It has set up no concentration camps, starved no enemies, practiced no cruelties.

Its battles have been for education, for the vote, for better working conditions… for safety on the streets… for child care, for social welfare… for rape crisis centers, women's refuges, reforms in the law.

If someone says, 'Oh, I'm not a feminist,' I ask, 'Why, what's your problem?

Dale Spender –
Man Made Language

Contents *Vol.10*

9 Introduction >> *Jessie Moss*

12 Voices of the tides: exploring feminism's fourth wave >> *Susanna Fiore*

18 An interview with Mani Mitchell >> *Mani Mitchell*

24 By their thousands: what Ada Byron knew >> *Melissa Chambers*

22 Technology & birth >> *Rosie Downing*

34 A tale of two mummies: >> *Huia Welton*

38 A kidnapping on Facebook >> *Marianne Bevan*

47 Sipping champagne in cyberspace >> *Felicity Scarce*

52 Say what? Feminist, queer and revolutionary vocabulary >> *Jessie Moss*

60 Filament series >> *Brie Sherow*

Contents Vol.10

Freeranger of the issue >> *Jessie Moss* **68**

Hey Girl: the faces and voices of the new online >> *Paula van Beek* **74**

Cheap'n' Choice: the Wikibomb >> *Byron Kinnaird* **84**

Beyoncé, Björk and Beats >> *Estère Dalton/Melody Thomas* **88**

Biographies of contributors >> **94**

Image credits >> **98**

Introduction
\>\>
Jessie Moss

Nau mai, haere mai ki te Freerange Vol. 10! Welcome, welcome, welcome one and all. *Feminism and technology wor(l)ds* shines two very bright lights on the themes it champions: feminism and technology. It looks at the state of our world through these lenses and considers how these two dynamic, essential and potentially disruptive spheres of thinking and doing interact – for better or for worse.

Technology has always been central to the human experience and has allowed us to evolve in to the people and societies we are today. Feminism, in its various iterations, has been in existence since the mid 1700s and is thought, action and a movement. Feminism is not singular, there are a multitude of forms it can take, which depend on the people who generate them. Feminism aims to speak truth to power – to create a just and equitable world. Technology seeks to change and advance the ways we interact with our physical world.

We are the makers of technology just as we are the constructors of our societies and the gender dynamics that structure them. The two are interrelated,

inseparable. Think of the power of a printing press and the dissemination of new and radical ideas; think birth control and reproductive technologies; think internet activism and solidarity. Although feminism considers certain technologies to be tools of positive change, it also examines those technologies that cause pain, suffering and destruction through oppression, control and disempowerment, and shows how these technologies can be dangerous weapons of the powerful.

I am proud to have curated this journal, to have provided this platform for many ideas, calls to action, proposals and questions. We are all fortunate to have this opportunity and do not take our relative freedoms for granted. Ten years ago I studied Gender and Women's Studies alongside Māori Studies (in the now defunct department at Victoria University of Wellington), and to this day get asked what that study is and what place it has in the world – to which I always answer: it is the study of half of the world's population, and actually the other half too. And more to the point, it is not as simple as a world of two halves. For gender (socially constructed roles and behaviours as well as the person individuals see themselves to be) and sex (the biological make up of individuals) both have many variations and intersections, which lead to the multitude of expressions of people the world over. This study has provided me with the tools to understand that history is contructed by those in power, that some people are oppressed for the benefit of others, that women are the working underclass of the world, that gender and sexual variation is still seen as sinful, that indigenous people and victims of war still struggle under colonialism and occupation, and that not all children are afforded the care, rights and protections they so need. With all of this in mind, I recognise that I am priviledged, and as such I have a distinct responsibility to show feminism in its breadth and depth as a force to be reckoned with.

Feminism and technology are two of the most powerful agents of change that we have. Here is how our contributors see it: Rosie Downing, Huia Welton and

Mani Mitchell provide insights into the equivocal status of technology and how it interacts physically with the human body in reproduction, childbirth and identity politics. Melody Thomas, Estère Dalton, Byron Kinnaird and Melissa Chambers explore how technology and those who control it can both hinder and advance careers and choices. From the first computer programmer in the world to broadcasters, beatmakers and the gatekeepers of knowledge, they explore the different places where feminism and technology meet. And who could fail to notice the ever present technology in our lives? Paula van Beek, Susanna Fiore, Felicity Scarce and Marianne Bevan all explore the effects, advances and changes that the internet and computers continue to have on feminism and the state of the world at large, whether it be the way women's self-esteem is constructed and assaulted daily by Facebook, Pinterest and blogs; how global solidarity for women can and can't be created and maintained in social media; how our young are now engaging with the fourth wave of feminism, which is inextricably connected to new technologies.

- Jessie Moss

Voices of the tides:
exploring feminism's fourth wave
>>
Susanna Fiore

Working as an actor in British theatre and television – neither industry being well known for its gender equality – has significantly developed my own relationship with feminism. As a teenager in the mid-1990s I was offered reductive 'girl power' courtesy of The Spice Girls, which reinforced the generally accepted social narrative of the time that we had entered a post-feminist era. This resulted in my coming out as a feminist fairly late in life. In 2008 I founded a theatre company with three other women and quickly realised that four women simply standing on stage together remains a rare sight in British theatre and could be viewed as a political act. Unlike our male peers, we were scrutinised and criticised on our politics with tired comments like 'Will you be burning your bras in your next production?' Again, unlike our male peers, our online presence has opened us up to ubiquitous sexually derogatory comments. I found I was ready to embrace the fourth wave of feminism.

The fourth wave is coming to be defined by, amongst other things, its intersectionality. The third wave, spurred on by bell hooks' book *Ain't I A Woman*, was seen as a reaction to the second wave's predominantly white and middle class focus. Like the third wave, the fourth wave considers other forms of oppression in addition to sexism such as race, class, sexuality and sexual identity. The key difference between these two movements is the way each is organised and communicated – the fourth wave's central nucleus being the internet. The internet is facilitating new globally accessible feminisms characterised by satirical humour in online content and an instantly reactive nature, which allows it to sit alongside and challenge or be challenged by other political issues of the day. It is also defined by its popularity and the sheer numbers of people engaging in multiple conversations on a myriad of feminist issues at any given moment. Where the third wave focused on emancipation of the individual, the fourth continues to permit the individual to affect change, but situates the individual as more of a starting point for this change.

I believe the fourth wave's defining feature is technology and its potential to reach a variety of different groups. To teenagers today, for example, the internet is simply another public space where they hang out. They read and engage with feminist issues online from the safety of their bedrooms, getting as involved as they choose, whether that means translating their ideas into campaigns at school (something I'm increasingly hearing about in the UK) or simply following a debate on Twitter. They are forming their worldview in a global, political context. This is where I see the greatest potential impact of the fourth wave: youth mobilised by feminism through technology.

Yet this technology could also be considered the fourth wave's limitation. That this wave hasn't yet amassed a lot of academic theory opens it up to criticism. According to Julia Schuster in 'Invisible Feminists?' it risks being considered a movement of the young, excluding those less technologically savvy. Her concern is also that many of the academics researching and publishing on feminism belong to an older age group and therefore academic feminism may risk overlooking the fourth wave. Each new wave could indeed be seen as a movement of the young. The technological nature of the fourth wave, however, can restrict access for many people, making it more explicitly a movement of the young. Maybe it is ok that this digital feminism has not yet found its academic feet. Its terminologies are still filtering through to general discourse, the perimeters around what denotes it as a 'wave' or 'movement' are still being discussed and it remains inclusive to non-academic feminists.

While this technology may currently exclude academic feminism, the fourth wave is nevertheless defined as being accessible because of it. Yet a peer of mine recently raised the point that because this wave is focused around those with access to technology, it is just as focused on first world values as the waves before it. However, one only has to start listing campaigns happening globally to contest this. Feminist group Femen in The Ukraine inspired Muslim Women Against Femen to take to the internet and dispute Femen's

This is where I see the greatest potential impact of the fourth wave: youth mobilised by feminism through technology.

focus. As an online-centred movement it can also encourage minimal political engagement. Whether signing a name on a petition, retweeting or composing a Facebook status, the medium demands little follow-through of its participants.

Some other flipsides to an instantly reactive medium are a culture of trolling and, at its most sinister, threats of rape and death aimed at women who speak out online for equality. Look no further than Caroline Craido-Perez who allegedly received 50 rape and death threats per hour for simply campaigning to have Jane Austin's image on a UK banknote in the name of positive female representation. It's hard not to feel the strength of the inherent dangers and prejudices against women who dare to have a public profile online.

tactics. Online forums have been used in recent years to aid marches in Nicaragua against domestic violence, in Afghanistan against stoning adulterers, and in Nepal, Pakistan and Bangladesh over gang rape. Its full global reach is questionable – there will always be people who have no access to the internet due to their location or their economic or educational status. Only time will tell as to whether such people will be reached out to indirectly by online campaigns.

Furthermore, the fourth wave risks depoliticisation with its focus on micropolitics and the frequent accusations of slacktivism levelled at it. There are a multitude of formal and informal groups and campaigns present across many different kinds of social media. It can make the wave seem quite sprawling and diluted in its political

The reoccurring question for me then is whether or not there truly is space for fourth wave feminism to prosper in this way? The more available it becomes, the more abuse, fear and misogyny it seems to generate. I see this backlash, however, as a necessary part of the movement. The Internet brings about some transparency to the levels of hatred and fear out there, so more feminists know what we are dealing with. Hopefully this also leads to ways of tackling it. I think backlashes and their retorts will ultimately bolster the movement because of the genuine openness of dialogue the Internet permits. In discussing fourth wave feminism, a reoccurring descriptive word is 'open'. Open in the sense that in principle it is all-inclusive, considers a matrix of discrimination and is made more accessible through online communities.

The fourth wave risks depoliticisation with its focus on micropolitics and the frequent accusations of slacktivism levelled at it.

Through galvanising activism, bringing together marginalised voices into a mainstream arena and opening up debate, the internet provides feminism with an everyday context. It allows the young who don't necessarily have such wide schemas of experience to join the debate. Although it hasn't yet garnered enough theoretical writing to give it academic legitimacy, it keeps avenues open for non-academic feminists to find their way. It exposes feminism to those who might otherwise choose to ignore it and is therefore likely to attract challenge and expose itself to denigration through trolling. It attracts further challenge by allowing people a noncommittal relationship with feminism, and yet it gives others a platform to affect real change. I think technology is what defines and yet makes fourth wave feminism polemic, but I am glad that these conversations are being had on this scale and I continue to follow its journey with anticipation.

Further recommended reading

Cochrane, Kira. *All The Rebel Women: The rise of the fourth wave of feminism.* GuardianShorts. 2013. E-Book.

Hooks, Bell. *Ain't I A Woman?* South End Press. 1981. Print.

Schuster, Julia. (2013) 'Invisible feminists? Social media and young women's political participation' *Political Science* Vol. 65, 8-24. June 2013. Sage Journals.

Mani Mitchell at an ILGA conference in Malta

An interview *with Mani Mitchell*

>>

Jessie Moss

Mani is a people's champion – a Waikato country kid born in the 1950s, now a counsellor, activist, educator and lecturer, and previously a manager at Regional Civil Defence. Assigned male and named Bruce at birth, then known as Margaret Ruth after exploratory surgery at age one, Mani now identifies as neither. Mani Bruce Mitchell is an intersex person, and a very hard working, informative, and open person at that. Thank you Mani for sharing with us.

JM: How do you define feminism and what does it mean to you?

MM: At its very best feminism is an analysis and movement that understands cis-male privilege, power dynamics and injustices for everyone who is not cis-male. For me, as an older person who was active in the 60s and 70s, it gave me an early framework for my activism and sense of the world.

JM: For those who have never heard the term 'intersex' – how would you explain it?

MM: Intersex is a medical umbrella term used for a variety of conditions in which a person is born with a reproductive or sexual anatomy that doesn't seem to fit the typical definitions of female or male.

JM: Prior to the medical interventions chosen for you at age eight, what understandings did you have of yourself?
MM: Due I imagine to trauma, I have very few memories of myself as a child. I knew I carried a terrible secret that I would not have been able to verbalise... I think I saw myself as a girl, probably a tomboy because that's what others may have said. I was a shy, country kid.

JM: In the 2010 film you created, *Intersexion*, Hamburg born Michel Reiter describes his parents' control and insistence on his various medical interventions as them 'collaborating with my enemies'. What was your perception of your situation and your parents' decisions as a child and young person?
MM: Fear.

JM: How did your constructed identity and associated narratives marry with your own emerging identity as time went on?
MM: There was nothing until my own melt down and then healing journey as a 40-year-old... Before that I was a paper mâché person who was very skilled at acting.

I could work out what was required for any given situation and simply act that. I made sure I never got close to people – no one would ever have known. The crazy part of all this was I myself did not know. We know what we know - that was my world, my reality. I had no sense that it was substantively different from other people's.

> *We know what we know - that was my world, my reality. I had no sense that it was substantively different from other people's.*
>
> *- Mani Mitchell*

It was only after entering my own therapeutic journey and exploration/search for my own story (discovering medical records, finding people who knew fragments of the story) that an authentic self-narrative emerged. This was a lengthy process that stretched over a number of years... In fact it took almost a decade.

JM: What was life like for people who didn't fit sexual and gender stereotypes during your Waikato University years? The time of Aotearoa's emerging social conscience?
MM: In those years I was doing everything to stay off radar and most people at that time would have seen me as 'normal female'. (I did not know who I was, so how could anyone else know?)

JM: How do you now negotiate a world where intersex identities are still rendered invisible by endless tick boxes, boys colleges, girls sports teams, barbies and clothing departments?
MM: Mostly I don't care. I know who I am, I live in a world where my reality is not validated, valued or recognised. Sometimes, like census night, I might make a statement – but mostly I don't bother – like many people who are minorities in a dominant culture, you do what you can to stay safe. My focus is my activism and I have a very long haul view of change.

JM: There are so many layers to an identity when you look at chromosomal sex, physical presentation and sexual orientation to name a few. In societies like New Zealand's, where binary, polarised constructions of male/female and masculine/feminine create dualities based on sexist social codes, rules and laws, what do you believe needs to be done to create space for everyone?
MM: Talk! Be different, and many of our youth are wonderfully doing just that...

JM: Globally, what has changed for intersex people since the 1950s?
MM: We have some visibility. We also have a significant body of academic thinking and writing on the issue; a small, growing body of research; an internationally networked activist community; a number of films and documentaries on the issue; a visibility and presence in places like WHO, HRC and the UN; the 'I' added to the GLBTI alphabet soup and conferences and retreats for intersex people.

On the flip side we have a very damaging nomenclature debate. In 2006 a group of mostly medical practitioners, a small number of intersex activists and academics met in Chicago to review the treatment protocols for intersex people. The hope was for a more person-centred model and a move away from stigma, shame and pathology. One result from that meeting was to change the medical umbrella term from intersex to DSD (disorders of sex development). The result was a massive ripping of the fledgling intersex movement. There was a sense that the community had been betrayed. At the time it was hoped this would radically improve the treatment of intersex people. Instead it seems to have reinforced the old paradigm of normalising. Rather than a step forward, it was a massive step backward. The nomenclature debate is on-going and has consumed huge amounts of activist energy and leads directly and indirectly to increased burn out and the loss of many people who had been involved in the movement.

Sadly it seems that the fears of those who disagreed with the 'new' term have been realised. Surgery has increased, not decreased. And while there have been some improvements in patient-centred care the vast majority of intersex 'patients' find their experience with doctors to be a negative rather than a positive one. So many people report not being listened to. Not being taken seriously.

Yet things are progressing. Consider the number of support organisations for adults and parents, and the International Lesbian, Gay, Bisexual, Trans and Intersex Association (ILGA) supported Malta forum. Then there is the growth of a very strong (vocal) youth run, intersex movement interACT. Finally, there are more and more out, intersex people holding leadership roles in various professional and academic organisations.

JM: What places are there for technology in intersex people's lives today?
MM: I have just come back from a meeting in Geneva, we made a statement that any process must involve us. So yes, if technology is being used to improve our individual quality of life, in a way that we are fully engaged and informed, then this can be a good thing.

We need to erase processes that continue to stigmatise, pathologise and normalise as these will continue the harm that has been done over the last century.

JM: What advice do you have for parents of intersex newborns?
MM: Not to panic. What your child needs most, you, as a parent, are very skilled and equipped to give: love, support and advocacy.

Take time, get support, reach out to the parent support groups that now exist around the world. Inform yourselves. Don't be rushed into making decisions you may later regret.

JM: Finally, does feminism champion intersex lives?
MM: Not in any cohesive, uniform way. However feminist-grounded organisations have been instrumental in providing leadership and very important support for intersex people to meet and discuss our issues. Foremost is ILGA, the world's oldest gay and lesbian organisation. It officially added 'I' to its name in 2008. ILGA sorted funding that enabled intersex activists to come together from all around the world for the first time ever. This group met three times in various locations (growing in size and global representation) to the last meeting in Malta where the nomenclature debate came to the fore.

And latterly the lesbian feminist organisation ASTRAEA has (after a parent donation) created a global fund to assist funding activism around the world. This is significant, as most of the work currently being done in the world (by intersex people) has not been funded.

If technology is being used to improve our individual quality of life, in a way that we are fully engaged and informed, then this can be a good thing.

By their thousands: *what Ada Byron knew*

>>

Melissa Chambers

Bletchley Park is full of secrets. Closed to visitors until the 1990s, the demure manor house grounds of the English wartime code-breaking compound resist disclosure of any kind. 'Keep it under your hat' a poster reads, 'Careless talk costs lives'. There's an actual hat depicted there, though not a fedora or a bowler. This one's a lady's hat.

At the height of World War II, 12,000 people contributed to the code breaking efforts at Bletchley. 8000 of them were women. Known as the Wrens, these women programmed and operated the machines that decrypted German, Italian and Japanese enemy intelligence, and reportedly shortened the war by up to four years. Along with everything about Bletchley, the Wrens' work and their very existence were silenced by the Official Secrets Acts until 1978.

Lift the hat further though and you discover that the Wrens were not alone. Concurrently in the United States, women at the University of Pennsylvania were setting up the Electronic Numerical Integrator and Computer (ENIAC), America's first electronic computing machine. Before the twentieth century masculinisation of the computer business, before the computer geeks, there were the computer girls. In fact almost all those working in computing until peace broke out were girls. With a few exceptions, even today their working lives remain undisclosed. At the time they were obliged not to say.

The intellectual life of a particular nineteenth century woman, however,

Before the twentieth century masculinisation of the computer business, before the computer geeks, there were the computer girls.

reaches across time to the Wrens and to us, and contrasts this non-disclosure. Ada Byron was an Englishwoman, an aristocrat, and by 1843 the world's first computational analyst. Her legacy is the earliest description of an algorithmic machine and the earliest account of a woman in computing. On the day I visit Bletchley, I wonder about Ada and the seemingly persistent invisibility of women working in technology today.

Ada was born in 1815 to the poet Lord Byron and mathematician Annabella Milbanke. In surely one of the briefest and worst marriages in history, romanticism and rationalism collided in the house of Byron to produce the first modern programmer with a foot in both camps. Ada grew up on maths. With her father banished to Italy, her mother raised her on a diet of numbers alone. Annabella was concerned with starving the poetic appetite that Ada might have inherited. She needn't have worried – Ada was a geek.

Luckily for her then (though dependent on the social and economic rank of your parents) the 1820s were a uniquely gender-blind time in terms of homeschooling in the sciences. For Ada this meant exposure to England's mathematical elite. And the best of this elite was Mary Somerville. Somerville is an interesting case – both in her own time and, for different reasons, ours. A self-taught scientist, polymath, mother and astronomer, Somerville was also a self-identified dark star in a male constellation. Though her epic legacy includes the coining of the term 'scientist', Somerville shrunk from public exposure and famously shrouded her gifts.

She claimed not to possess genius for 'that spark from heaven is not granted to the sex' (Winter 207) – rather she saw herself as capable only of perseverance. When she became the first woman member of the Royal Astronomical Society, she declined the invitation to attend the inauguration. In fear of embarrassing the men, she sent apologies with her husband and continued to teach Ada.

At this time, the English mathematical community raced to catch up with its continental counterparts. Leading this charge was Charles Babbage. Babbage had an idea to mechanise calculus. And Babbage was thinking big.

In the science museum in London today, you can visit Babbage's Difference Engine, only built after his death. You can also visit his brain. Next to the machine and under his brain is his day book. In 1843 it records the day when the Lady Ada Byron (by now, the married Lady Lovelace) attended to discuss what are known as her notes.

These notes are Ada's only legacy – she died nine years later at the age of 36. They are her remarks on the Analytical Engine. For Ada and Babbage this was the next logical step from the Difference Engine; for us it is the first general-purpose computer.

Out of the crash of poetry and logic, she was the one that said 'Don't you see?'

In these notes we find the earliest interpretation of algorithmic technology, pre-dating Alan Turing and the Wrens by 100 years. Babbage was a curmudgeon, famous for designing engines no one would build. Ada was a visionary, she saw the potential of a machine that could convert numbers into symbols. She said that one day someone would design a general principle to govern this kind of system and that this would be applied not only to mathematical abstraction but to art, music and communication. Out of the crash of poetry and logic, she was the one that said 'Don't you see?'

I am a theatre director. I try to tell stories that matter. When I first read about Ada I knew it was a good story and was sure I knew why. At first I thought this was because it showcased an intellectual robbed by the social code of her time, that her real impact was misplaced for over a century in a history mediated by powerful men.

Now, though, I see I got that wrong. Her legacy was misplaced only because she died young. Ada didn't keep what she did a secret at the time, not as Somerville did. And it's this tendency by women towards secreting their achievements in male dominated professions that adds dimension to the persistently clandestine legacy of the Wrens.

In reading Ada's personal letters (as published in *Ada, the Enchantress of Numbers*), you meet a person not only of extreme skill, but one given to self-disclosure, insistence and lack of apology. In a vacuum of women speaking publicly on mathematics, she wrote to Charles Babbage and chided his inaccuracies. While Somerville said that her mind was not capable of creative logic, Ada counted her ideas as the ones that mattered. She was a secret to no one, especially herself. She was the future in more ways than one.

The history of women in computers catches people off guard today. While the 50-year silence on the nature of the work at Bletchley and the 8,000 women engaged in it was broken in the 70s, it is still seen as revolutionary when a female mathematician wins the Fields Medal. Why? It is seen as revolutionary to be a woman with skill enough to code for Google. Why, when programmers were mostly women to begin with? The computing workforce during the war could be seen as circumstantially female. And it was. But it was also shot through with brilliance, innovation and skill. It could also be seen as only circumstantially secret, but I think this still sounds a warning in a time where a strong narrative on women's ability to lead in the technology business is urgently needed.

A 2004 study by the National Center for Women and Information technology (NCWIT) found that women already employed in the technology industry are leaving at staggering rates. Given the aggressive sexism of the programming business today, it is no wonder that, despite their antecedents, contemporary women who are gifted in the computational sciences tend to assume Somerville's posture and keep it under their hats.

But there is no chromosome for innovation. And the next Ada could be anywhere. Standing on the grass at Bletchley, I remember them – the women and girls by their thousands working at a time when no one knew where this thinking would take us. But Ada did and would have done it herself if she had lived. And so I think that even today, when you are a woman, what you are doing can be as secret as you like, and maybe it needs be. That you are doing it though needs to be shouted out loud. From Ada, to the Wrens, to the ENIAC girls, the impact of women in computing through time is already there if you look for it.

Don't you see? The secret's out.

'Ada Lovelace 1838' aka Ada Byron by William Henry Mote

Works cited

Tool, Betty A. A*da, the Enchantress of Numbers: Prophet of the Computer Age.* Strawberry Press, 1998. Print.

Winter, Alison. 'A Calculus of Suffering.' *Science Incarnate: Historical Embodiments of Natural Knowledge.* Eds Christopher Lawrence & Steven Shapin. Chicago: University of Chicago Press, 1998. Print.

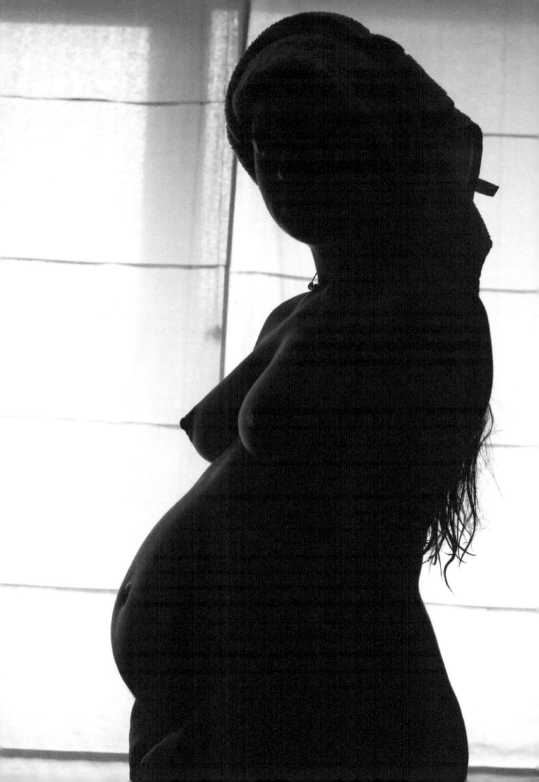

Technology & birth

>> Rosie Downing

Around the world, countless women and their families will celebrate the birth of their baby. This is not a new experience; women have always birthed, often with the support of experienced and knowledgeable (usually female) birth attendants, using natural aids. In the last century women, their babies and families have been increasingly expected to engage with, and utilise, technological input and interventions in their pregnancies and births. While this has contributed to the significant improvement in infant and maternal morbidity and mortality rates worldwide, there are other inherent risks, such as the loss of traditional birthing knowledge and practices, women feeling disempowered and not in control of their bodies, and a significantly narrowed understanding of 'normal' birth. I would argue that as we engage with technology during pregnancy and birth, there are

Technological involvement in pregnancy and birth risks the perpetuation of a 'guilty until proven innocent' approach to screening and care provision, where the default understanding of women's bodies is that they are weak, untrustworthy and vulnerable rather than capable, versatile and resilient.

some considerations and potential risks worth discussing if we are to ensure that technology remains a beneficial tool and an aid to women, their families and the processes of pregnancy and birth.

Invaluable skills and traditions around keeping pregnancy and birth healthy have been developed over many thousands of years. These practices have come about through observing women's health, behaviour and wellbeing. For example, assessing the difference between fluid retention and other normal changes in pregnancy and potentially fatal pre-eclampsia and oedema. Consider the knowledge acquired over time around preventative care and subtle but safe interventions, such as turning breech babies. Consider the interpersonal skills that can significantly enhance education and safety for both mother and baby. If we were to lose these skills, we would lose the cumulative knowledge gathered over countless generations, and it would be nearly impossible to regain it. It only takes disruption between one generation and the next for the transmission of knowledge to cease.

Technology isn't infallible. You only need to have worked as a maternity carer through one black-out or have needed the only specialist-trained technician who happens to be unavailable at the time, to appreciate that reality. Midwife and activist Ina May Gaskin tells a story of a woman in North America who went for elective caesarean section only for the doctors in the operating theatre to discover she was not pregnant, rather severely constipated. Evidently, in the absence of abdominal palpation (a low-tech skill) and basic assessment of pregnancy, the ultrasounds she attended in her 'pregnancy' were of course, as Ina May reminds us, 'only as good as the person reading it'. Technology itself cannot care for and ensure the health of women and babies; we need skilled humans who understand and can work with the nuances and complexities of the human mind and body.

A more subtle risk I see is the undermining and disempowerment of important familial roles, social structures, and women's own control and belief in their bodies, and perhaps most importantly, their confidence in themselves as mothers. As we increasingly shift our discourses around pregnancy and birth to focus on the risks and fears, rather than the normalcy and celebration of pregnancy and birth, what message are we sending to our societies as a whole? Holly Priddis et al., among other researchers, have investigated this scenario. In their work, analysis of women's own narration and language as they told their birth stories and of the medical care they received for a specific condition revealed common themes of: 'I am broken and a failure', and 'dismissed, devalued and disregarded'. They concluded in their paper that although the condition itself may well have significant impact on the women's identity and wellbeing, 'health professionals should be mindful of the language that they use and their actions… to avoid causing unnecessary distress'. Technological involvement in pregnancy and birth risks the perpetuation of a 'guilty until proven innocent' approach to screening and care provision, where the default understanding of women's bodies is that they are weak, untrustworthy and vulnerable rather than capable, versatile and resilient. A greater risk still, is if women begin to believe this of their own bodies.

At this point in time with the available technology, if we believe that every birth needs to be technologically monitored in order to be safe, this means that it must happen in the hospital setting – away from the comfort and safety of home and the support and involvement of broader family and community. Birth risks becoming something that we only hear about or see edited versions of. What then becomes of the roles that partners and the wider family previously held?

In Puvirnituq, Nunavik (in far northern Canada), the community has fought to keep birthing in their community, knowing that they have limited access to advanced technologies. As one elder explains in J Stonnier's work: 'You can't have a community where the biggest event is death. There is a beginning and an end to life. We need to know both.' I don't have any simple answers, but to me, this begs the question: if we unintentionally turn this rite of passage and celebration into a process that risks making women and their families feel disempowered, fearful and weak, what are we losing? What do we risk erasing from our social fabric and future generations?

If we replace our confidence in our bodies with assurances sought from machines, and our knowledge of natural processes with statistically defined normalcy, not only do we risk undermining and limiting our skills, ourselves and our identities, we also risk narrowing our definition and understanding of 'normal' and subsequently, 'safe'. There are as many versions of 'normal and safe' pregnancies and births as there are women in the world. If we strive to ensure that each pregnancy and birth fits an unquestioned predefined notion of 'normal and safe' (for example, without consideration of her context, or own definition), we risk unnecessarily interfering with a natural process, potentially doing more harm than good.

I believe however, that there are ways for high- and low-tech practices to co-exist and for women and their babies to get the best from both worlds. To achieve this we must take the time to consider the roles, strengths and weaknesses and implications of each, rather than rushing to accept technological advances simply because they exist. We also need to make use of the inherent strengths and knowledge of their bodies that women have, the community support networks and traditional knowledge bases. To balance the risks with the obvious benefits that technology can bring, we need to consider its use in individualised contexts and with fully informed consent. Only then will technology truly contribute to the complete health and wellbeing of women and their families.

Works cited

Priddis, Holly, Hannah Dahlen and Virginia Schmied. "Women's experiences following severe perineal trauma: a meta-ethnographic synthesis." *Journal of Advanced Nursing.* ResearchGate, 10 Oct. 2012. Web.

Stonnier J et al. "To Bring Birth Back is to Bring Back Life: the Nunavik Story." *Maternity Care Models on the Edge.* Ed. RD Floyd. In publication 2015.

The Face of Birth."Face of Birth Experts - Ina May Gaskin on the loss of essential knowledge of natural birth." Online video clip. *YouTube.* YouTube, 29 Oct. 2011. Web. May 2015.

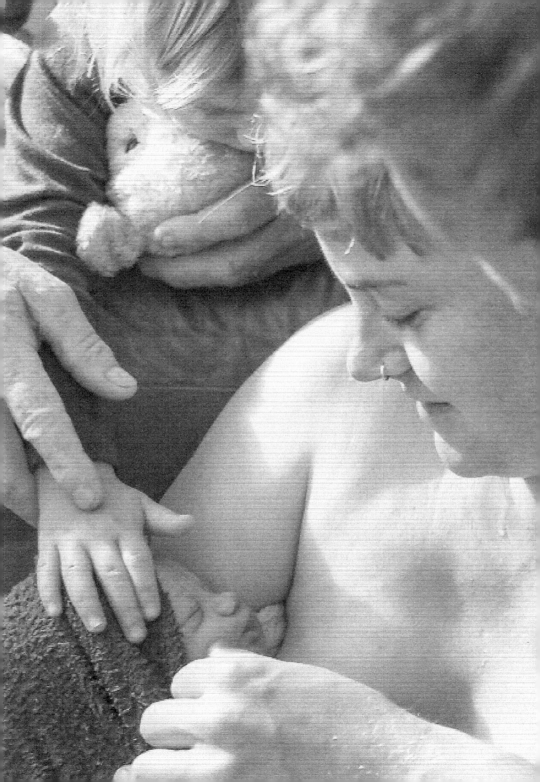

'You can't have a community where the biggest event is death. There is a beginning and an end to life. We need to know both.'

A tale of two mummies: *no penis involved in the making of this baby* >>

Huia Welton

Parenting is a wild ride. Seriously. It means caring for another human being twenty-four hours a day, seven days a week, often while solving problems with not much more than guess work and tears (the child's and yours). It's stressful and scary and I am so not the parent I thought I would be. All parents, regardless of sexual orientation, have challenges. Having been out for over fifteen years – more than 50 per cent of my life – it's safe to say that I'm pretty secure in my sexuality and the occurrences of having to come out again (in the sense of defending who I am) have since become few and far between. Then came parenting. Parenting with another woman (an amazing woman it has to be said), I am refreshed that we have no gender-based conventions or traditional (and sexist) role expectations to meet The assumption that men and women who create relationships and babies together are the normal standard and that all other forms of families and indeed sexualities are deviations or abnormalities is sometimes a challenge for us and reminder of how far our society has to go.

Breeding may well have a strong association with the heteros but dykes can do it too. One of the stranger experiences I've had was bumping into someone from my past, a member of our local community, who assumed that because I was now a mumma that meant I'd therefore given up on pussy. No penis was used in the making of our baby (we conceived using an anonymous donor sperm from Fertility Associates). It was a strange experience, having to reassure

> *The assumption is always that our son has a dad – that he must just be elsewhere at any (every) given moment.*

that, yes I am still lesbian and yes our baby has two mummies. We've certainly learnt to expect that the straights need educating – but it's tedious and exasperating to receive such reactions from our own community.

The assumption is always that our son has a dad – that he must just be elsewhere at any (every) given moment. Health professionals, coffee groups, other parents, old ladies in supermarkets, swimming class instructors and retail workers all assume a man must be in our family and refer to 'daddy' and 'husband' with more frequency than I would have thought possible. Just the other week we took our boy to the after hours medical centre. The nurse wanted to know which of us was the mother; the doctor asked the same question. They looked startled, surprised when told that 'We're both his mothers'. There was no negativity in their reaction - the female doctor even said 'Oh... lovely' - but the invisibility of our family unit is wearying. If we were a couple of straights the question wouldn't have been asked and our family unit would be accepted on sight. Man + woman + baby = family. This is what they ask us outloud, but what they are asking is: where is the father? Where is the male role model? Not only does this reduce our status as parents, it says a lot

Being well-schooled in the expectations of our society, our same-sex parenting community knows that the value of a parent isn't defined by something so simple. Parenting is about the constant ongoing love, attention, care and nurturing a child requires, not about the parents' genders.

about how we as a society view ourselves. Do we really think that families live in such isolation that they aren't exposed to role models of all ilks, genders and sizes, who are able to model and teach many different behaviours and skills? This confined thinking perpetuates the cycle of what it is to be a boy, a girl, a person and restricts the possibilities of what can be for children.

For this reason, we feel a really strong responsibility to ensure that our boy has exposure to other families that look like his. We are fortunate that the queer community in Wellington has an established 'Pride and Joy' playgroup. Online queer parenting communities also provide valued soildarity. Rainbow Families NZ is a Facebook group that provides a great space to talk about everything from our experiences using fertility clinics to kids books that reflect our families. Being a queer parent is different from being a straight parent because our society is so fixated with biological connection between parent and child. This is seen as the validator of significance. Being well-schooled in the expectations of our society, our same-sex parenting community knows that the value of a parent isn't defined by something so simple. Parenting is about the constant ongoing love, attention, care and nurturing a child requires, not about the parents' genders.

For the record our son doesn't have a dad. He has a donor. He also has two devoted mummies who love each other and him to the moon and back.

A kidnapping *on Facebook*

>>

Marianne Bevan

As I write it's **17 April 2015.** It's now been 367 days since the Chibok girls were kidnapped in Nigeria. After they were taken, their physical absence was contrasted with their online presence; their names and pictures circulated around the internet as people grappled with how to get them back.

This constant online visibility has since ceased and aside from a casual appearance every month or so decrying the amount of time they have been away, international demands for their return appear to have ceased. Only those more closely connected to the girls are still talking about their return.

On 15 April 2014, 276 girls gathered to take their final physics exam at their high school in Chibok. They were taken by Boko Haram, a terrorist group operating in Nigeria. This event was shocking in its brutality and symbolism, but it was just one in a string of equally troubling attacks committed over the past several years by the group. At the time, the Nigerian military was in the process of trying to rid the region of Boko Haram, amidst stories of human rights abuses from both sides.

Initiated by women in Nigeria, protests quickly started against the kidnapping. The protests were largely directed at the Nigerian government, at their reluctance to take action and their broader failures of governance. This awareness-raising was instigated by women on the ground who knew the context and the issues, who lived them daily. The protests continued to spread via women in the diaspora across the world.

It was through Facebook that I first heard about what had happened – the news getting to me from friends in the region who I had worked with in Ghana on girls' rights, militarism and peace-building.

For a while, the Western media payed little attention to what had happened. Several weeks later, the #bringbackourgirls hashtag began and swept across the internet. Profile pictures of people holding bringbackourgirls signs spread with Emma Watson, Michelle Obama, Michael Bolton and Reese Witherspoon all endorsing the cause.

As the hashtag spread, criticisms of neo-colonialism came from a range of feminist and post-colonial commentators. There was concern that this was another case of a complicated situation becoming simplified by Western media and others who previously knew nothing about Boko Haram and the broader political context in Nigeria. There were also fears that calls to 'Do something!' could encourage a Nigerian or foreign military operation, the risks of which would be high when the last thing that was needed was increased militarisation in the area. There was also concern that the 'our' in the hashtag suggested an ownership over these girls that very few in the West could lay claim to.

Teju Cole, a Nigerian novelist started to tweet about these concerns. He made a distinction between the two sides of the campaign, encapsulating many of the criticisms of the diverging directions it had taken: 'Remember: #bringbackourgirls, a vital moment for Nigerian democracy, is not the same as #bringbackourgirls, a wave of global sentimentality.'

The impact of conflict on women and girls continually fails to be given the attention it deserves by international media.

As these criticisms continued, the West African woman kept on protesting; many of them were using the slogan. There was a photo of the girls we had worked with in Nkwanta, Northern Ghana, holding bringbackourgirls signs – girls who face all manner of injustices on a daily basis. There was a protest in Monrovia, Liberia, under the title of 'They are our girls too', where girls held up bringbackourgirls signs, girls who, if not old enough to remember the Liberian war, continue to live with its effects. Leymah Gbowee, the Liberian activist and Nobel Peace Prize winner, started speaking out about how this was another example of action taken by women in the face of conflict and injustice, and the need to keep remembering that.

Chibok girls school uniforms
Opposite page: Dress owned by an abducted school girl

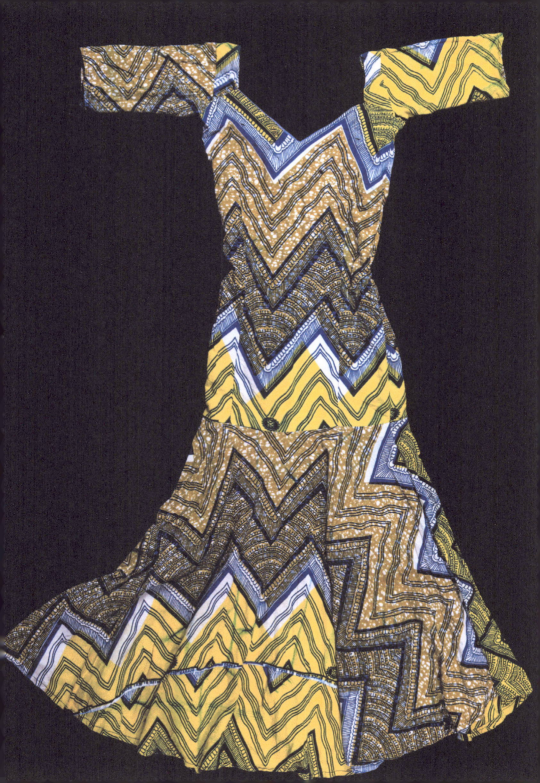

Some of the girls

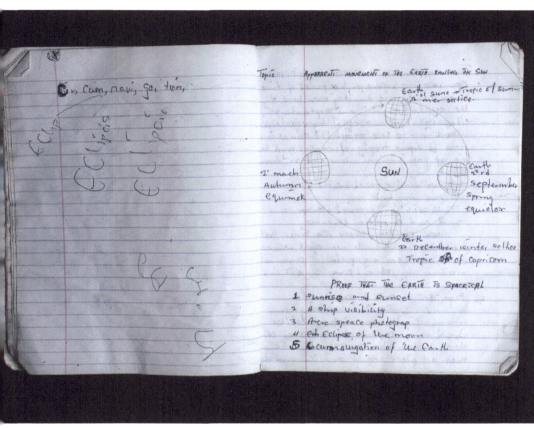

School text book

In New Zealand, someone organised a protest and I thought about whether or not to go. There was a reasonable level of support although criticisms of neo-colonialism on the Facebook posts advertising it started coming in. Had this been several years ago, before I had spent time in West Africa, perhaps I would have been too concerned about it being an ineffectual and possibly damaging campaign (in the ways critics have identified above) and may not have gone to the protest. But for me, there were relationships I needed to honour: to not attend a protest that was in some way similar to those being organised and attended by friends in the region would have felt like a betrayal to my friends over there and to the work we had been doing. It was these women's lead I was trying to follow, so I went. Someone else responded to these Facebook criticisms by saying she was going to support one of the organisers of the protest, a woman who was from the region. Perhaps for her too, not going would have been a betrayal of friendship.

Some might say that I was getting too caught up in a singular emotional response to an event while losing sight of the wider politics of the situation and my place within it. But I think that's a false division, which ignores the complexities of transnational links and relationships, and the benefits that can be derived from these. The impact of conflict on women and girls continually fails to be given the attention it deserves by international media. It was through this campaign that the issue was brought to the attention of government bodies in a way that was difficult to ignore; social media was

...social media was being used in a way that made women more difficult to ignore – the situation of the kidnapped girls made it into the international media and prompted calls for action.

being used in a way that made women more difficult to ignore – the situation of the kidnapped girls made it into the international media and prompted calls for action. This opened space for solidarity and we have feminists who use technology to thank for this. Of course, how the technology is engaged with, and by whom, is what determines the quality of this solidarity.

There are often criticisms of how women from the West engage with feminist issues in the Global South: that when criticising poverty, inequality and militarization in foreign countries, we often fail to address the West's wider complicity in creating and sustaining these issues through colonialism and the continuation of unequal international political and economic systems; that we fail to recognise the often pressing issues caused by unequal gender, class and racial structures at home. It was the perpetuation of these exact issues that many of the Western feminists critiquing #bringbackourgirls were – rightly – concerned about.

However, this campaign was started by women in Nigeria and sustained by women throughout West Africa and the diaspora. One of the long-term impacts of colonialism and patriarchy has been to silence and sideline African women who have played instrumental roles in political action and peace-building. As images of Nigerian women leading these protests started coming out, it seemed that this time women would start getting the recognition for the action they were leading, as they were identified as the initiators of the campaign. In this situation, to listen to these Nigerian women and to amplify their opinions and solutions is to challenge the legacies of colonialism.

I worry that as the campaign started to be critiqued, the space they had carved out to talk was not recognised and was inadvertently diminished. This is not to say that people should have engaged in a superficial way with the campaign – by changing their profile pictures and attending protests without thinking critically about the impact of their actions. Instead they needed to support the women who initiated the protest and are battling their own governments to ensure that peaceful solutions are found. This is a means to negate uninformed foreigners calling for increased militarisation in the area in response to protests. This makes the priorities of those directly affected more likely to be addressed and avoids damage that can occur when foreign governments try to impose solutions from the outside.

A long time before Facebook was around, bell hooks said: 'Solidarity is not the same as support. To experience solidarity we must have a community of interests, shared beliefs and goals around which to unite, to build sisterhood … solidarity requires sustained, ongoing commitment' (65). After the international recognition peaked, the slogan started to die out. People's profile pictures were changed. The international protests stopped. In many ways then, the critics were probably right: for a lot of people outside the region, the campaign was a trend and while people's sense of outrage was no doubt genuine, it was fleeting and that's not enough to sustain a movement.

It was more a show of support, of pictures on computer screens rather than active attempts to support local voices, of building on existing networks and linking to broader goals and campaigns for gender equality and peace. This is one of the problems with trying to use social media to build feminist solidarity. Without the everyday, face-to-face interactions that come with traditional campaigning, there's less chance that strong connections to the movement will develop and it is easy for people to forget about it.

While the urging to 'act local' and focus on issues within your own country is valid, I worry that sometimes it ignores the way that events far away are connected to people and events at home. These incidents do not just affect those in the immediate vicinity but they spread out in complex webs to Nigerians in New Zealand, West Africans in America and African-American's in America. If there is someone who is Nigerian in New Zealand who is hurt by this, then solidarity means to support her and her networks.

One of the long-term impacts of colonialism and patriarchy has been to silence and sideline African women who have played instrumental roles in political action and peace-building.

The point is not to say that one form of solidarity, be it face-to-face or through social media, is better than the other, but rather that they rely on each other so much that we need to focus on their connections rather than their divisions. Beneath the surface of bringbackourgirls campaign, this was going on, and critics possibly just didn't see it as they became more concerned with critique and possible divisions. Solidarity is not just actions to change government policy and practice, but it is the intimate gestures and emotional support we give to friends. It is often these small gestures that get lost when we try to dissect campaigns, but it is these that solidarity is often built on and from which it flourishes.

Works cited

Cole, Teju (RealityVirtual). "Remember: #bringbackourgirls, a vital moment for Nigerian democracy, is not the same as #bringbackourgirls, a wave of global sentimentality." 8 May 2014, 8:36 a.m. Tweet.

Hooks, bell. *Feminist Theory: From Margin to Centre.* New York: Pluto Press, 2000. Print.

Sipping *champagne In cyberspace*
>>
Felicity Scarce

have always been a casual documenter, jotting down lines when the mood takes me. A few years ago, on the upswing from a lengthy period of serious depression, I started writing more seriously. It became a ritual, a spirited one after so long horizontal. I spent a summer writing at my desk late into the night, feeding recycled brown paper into the typewriter. I wore a black lace bra and listened to Tallulah, songs of heroines, by local Brisbane band The Go-Betweens. I drank red wine from a jar for fortitude, romance, and (I thought) a bit of extra nous.

More recently I've taken part in an online writing course for women. The course encouraged healing and boldness through transforming narratives, so was a natural progression from my first ceremony of remedial and celebratory writing. Part of the programme's daily practice was to engage with a Facebook community. Using Facebook as a platform was an intentional choice on the part of the facilitator, who aimed to highlight the clamouring for validation it fosters and the insecurity it breeds when we don't receive this. For me it wasn't about the likes, it was about my perception of other women and the way this clouds my self-image. There are things I pluck from someone's online presence to chastise myself with: their art projects, their suave application of eyeliner, their bold pattern-clashing outfits, their attractive friends. These are all things I possess (the eyeliner is a work in progress). But I have been trained as an expert in self-judgement. Our patriarchal society normalises comparison, encouraging women to compete with each other. In turn I can tear myself apart in a split second. I am not flawless, fashionable, and ultimately, feminine, enough.

As proud as I was of the writing I created and shared during this course, there were times when I merged the work of other women with the ephemeral fragments of their beings – all gleaned from their online presence – and used this blend to make myself feel small and dusty. I can project whole films about other women in which I, the director, am merely a flat shadow hanging behind their glow. I use the internet – a tool for connection – to sever my ties to women who are just like me: sitting behind their computer screens, chewing on their own judgement. I don't see our commonality, our shared vulnerability. I only see my lack. Cutting ourselves down is the same as cutting other women down. What we project toward ourselves has the most significance.

I trawl the scene for body parts. My eyes always flit to other women's legs – my Achilles heel in my own bodily self-acceptance.

I use the poems I write for the course as a weapon against this perception of myself – a mangled image, informed by a tangle of outside influences and loaded with self-criticism. I return to my own tool of power – writing – to reclaim a different version of the stories I have told myself. The familiar alchemy of ink on a blank page makes the unseen visible; it digs up shame, dries it out. I look at the dips of my body as oceans, not muggy swamps in a drought. I write stories where women brag; I know anyone can crush themselves like I can. I celebrate gifts.

I don't want to preserve myself from the internet. I want to cultivate self-control in how I engage. To use the space to celebrate, to clink glasses.

I use the internet – a tool for connection – to sever my ties to women who are just like me: sitting behind their computer screens, chewing on their own judgement. I don't see our commonality, our shared vulnerability. I only see my lack.

Bottle

I

My dad had no mortal father
but he had a heavenly one.
At dinner time when we all sat and talked
so my parents could spare us the pain of
their fragmented upbringings
god was served onto my plate
it was all my father could cook
and god made me swallow shame and
guilt
until they took over my white blood cell
count
until my body was bagged
and I wonder if god is what gave my
sisters and I a dangerous devotion to the
blues in our veins
(and I don't mean money)
or if we got this from our grandmothers.
And all we got from grandfathers is
an empty cup.

II

It is whisky that connects me to the woman who was my first home. A map of the cold south, it is undeniable lineage that we were raised to forgive, because for all the garbage there was love lifted and toasted and drunk every morning, every night.

III

It is whisky – a grandmother's salvation, a mother's medicine – that is my family heirloom, the only glowing artefact. I drink it on the rocks with my sister at sunset to warm the streets of her cold new town. Friends carry it like gold to the manger marked by constellations of tears. I drink it with my beloved, for memory, for grief. With kin we pour one out. An amber spirit worn by babes, strength against a painful bite, I too am teething, against my chest these jewels strung by my ancestors, I draw with words a path to a flame that embraces my family in mourning, a gilded arrow woven through my ribcage, fierce as them I breathe.

Sites

When I think of my body
I think of tiny sites
nipples, dimples, fingernails,
the space inside the caves.

But the place that calls to me,
monumental, ground onto earth
are twin towers
thighs that bark
trunks to hold stars

Carriage for treasure
on board my body,
this floating tenement.

These vessels
pelted with hail
soft like a fox worn across shoulders,
that kind of softness
that is hard to look at.

The river bears the same blue neon road
that is tattooed across my body
The crevices of the moon
are the same place.
The story held is weathered
one chipped piece of tile from a roadside
shrine

It has travelled no distance.
It has just been picked up,
rubbed under thumb,
and like a click
become a talisman that can be
pocketed
to call out this magic in any place

Say what?

Say what?

Say what?

Say what?

Feminist, queer & revolutionary vocabulary

Jessie Moss

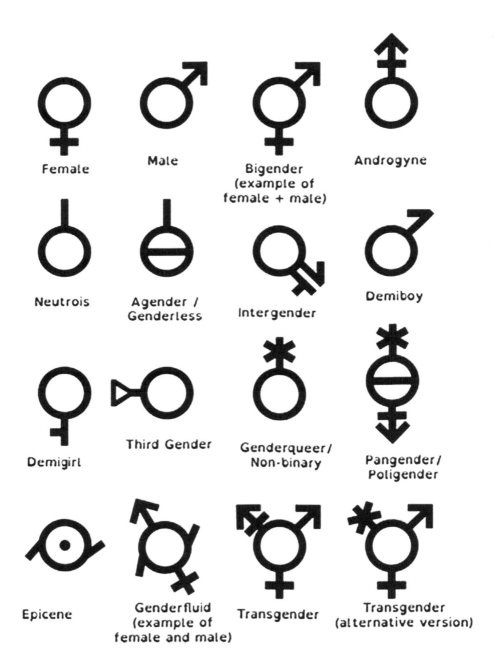

Feminism

Some say it is about the equality or equity of the sexes, but when 'sex' isn't that simple – and there is more than 'man' and 'woman' in this world – you see that feminism is rather complex! It is a movement and analysis that recognises the inseparable combinations that exist between patriarchy, cis-male ('status quo-male') privilege, capitalism, homophobia and white privilege to name a few. It is the knowledge that these combinations form political, social and economic power structures, which create injustices for and oppress non cis-male people. Feminism is a lens in which to view and understand the world – a vehicle for change.

Patriarchy

Patriarchy describes male-dominated power structures, which permeate throughout organised society, in political systems as well as in individual relationships. It is systemic bias against women and non cis-male people. Patriarchy can be recognised as the institutions and companies that are run in the majority by men that mostly benefit men; where taking maternity leave or breastfeeding a baby at work is a problem; where being a transsexual makes using the toilets an issue. Patriarchy is also a family group or community controlled by powerful men - fathers and grandfathers who give more privilege to boys and men in that group. Patriarchy is a world that benefits cis-men over everyone else.

Gender essentialism

Gender essentialism is such a commonly held belief that most people wouldn't know they hold it. It drives many unconscious behaviours and forms the basis of most patriarchal, misogynistic and sexist actions, arguments and discussions. It is the basic idea that men and women act in inherently different ways and as such have different options in life because of intrinsic biological differences between the genders.

Gender essentialism often excuses gender-based oppressions and discriminations in societies, such as what roles parents play, what jobs people hold, expectations held of each other and skill bases. Gender essentialism simultaneously reinforces gender stereotypes, while being informed by them. Gender essentialism relies on the perpetuation of a binary, polarised world, free of ambiguity, where two neat tidy genders exist and know their place in the world.

Cisgender, cissexual

'Cis' (pronounced 'sis') is Latin for 'on the side of' and is the antonym to 'trans' meaning 'on the other side/across from'. Cis-male and cis-female people are those who feel there is a match between their assigned birth sex and the gender they feel themselves to be, in contrast to transsexual people. The term was created so cis-men and cis-women aren't seen as the normal standard from which everyone else deviates, whereby people such as transsexuals and LBGTIQ would be viewed as abnormal.

LGBT - LGBTI - LGBTIQ

These initials mean 'Lesbian, Gay, Bisexual, Transgender, Intersex, Queer', and represent the diversity in sexualities, genders and cultures that are subject to discrimination, persecution and violence globally. They can also be used to refer to someone who is non-heterosexual/cis-gendered.

Intersex
To quote Mani Mitchell: 'Intersex is a medical umbrella term used for a variety of conditions in which a person is born with a reproductive or sexual anatomy that doesn't seem to fit the typical definitions of female or male.'

Misogyny
A dislike, ingrained prejudice and/or contempt of women which can manifest in numerous ways, including sexual discrimination, violence against women and the sexual objectification of women.

Oppressed, repressed or supressed?
To oppress is to keep a person or group powerless by unjust force or authority. To repress is to hold back by coercion, or hold down by force. Suppression means to put an end to, to inhibit, and to keep from being revealed (knowledge or recognition for example). These are some of patriarchy's best-prized tools in the power tool kit.

Discrimination
The unjust or prejudicial treatment of different groups of people, usually based on the grounds of race, age, or sex or sexuality.

First wave feminism
Feminism initially emerged from the Western world to the backdrop of the age of the Enlightenment (1650s – 1780s) when analysis, reason and the individualistic thinking of philosophers and scientists challenged traditional authorities of the Church and Throne. Debates around women, colonialism and slavery abound, however women were almost entirely kept from the table, creating a pro-male movement. Then came the intense industrialisation of the West in the 1800s, starting in Europe. For women this meant further burden in addition to childbearing and mammoth Victorian work loads running small holdings and households. Women and children now also worked in factories and businesses, but had none of the rights afforded to men to safeguard their working conditions, politics of the day or land and sexual rights.

Fed up with their lot, women of the Commonwealth and North America demanded change. The defining struggle for the first wave was women winning the battle for the vote. The suffragette movement officially started in the USA at the Seneca Falls Convention, 1848, but New Zealand was the first country where all women could vote in 1893, followed by the USA in 1920 and Britain in 1928. This was feminism by and for the white middle and upper-class women and their families. For this reason the second wave was born.

Second wave feminism
Loosely framed by the civil rights movement and anti-Vietnam War protests of the 1960s through to the neoliberal politics of the 1980s and 1990s, the second wave sought emancipation and equality for women on the basis of economics, sexuality and politics. There was a growing recognition of the multiple oppressions and battles that women faced in this wave. Where black women, lesbian women and

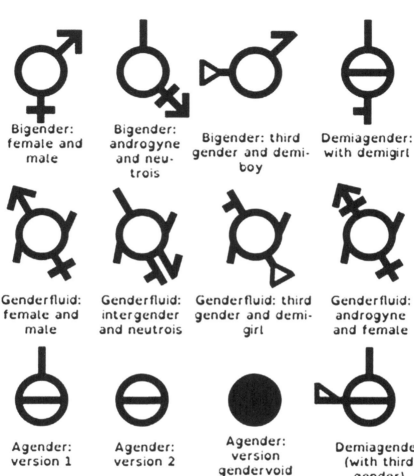

indigenous women from all around the world had been left out of the equation, there was now some representation for them in feminism. Connections were made between broad political structures such as capitalism, war, patriarchy and heteronormativity, as well as the roles of women as wives and mothers. Sex and gender were differentiated as a biological base and social constructs respectively. Sexuality and reproductive rights became central issues. The women's struggle was associated with the class struggle, the personal was now political, and everyone was invited to bang a drum on the march.

Third wave feminism
Although many legal and institutional rights had now been granted to women as a result of the second wave, the 1990s children of the second wave feminists had something else to say. Informed by post-colonial and post-modern thinking, they wanted changes in media representation of women and of gender stereotyping. The focus shifted from what was good for all women, based on the personal being political, to 'micro-politics', where women were encouraged to use their own personal identities to define what being a feminist meant to them. A woman could wear lipstick and high heels, run a boardroom and still be a feminist. Language such as 'slut' and 'bitch', deemed misogynistic in the second wave, was reclaimed in order to suffocate sexist language.

The fourth wave
Has it arrived and when? It is differentiated from its predecessors by its use of the internet. The fourth wave's creation-in-action is evidenced online in forums, blogs, social media and clicktavism causes. The third wave's increasing intersectionality has brought all sorts of individuals and groups into the frame and to the screen. There is no one experience, no one feminism. However, the fourth wave also looks back to the second to inform its arguments about the state of the world, a world controlled by patriarchal capitalists and run by the West, taking into account issues such as climate change, severe poverty and systemic racism.

Intersectionality
Intersectionality describes the ways in which oppressive institutions (racism, homophobia, transphobia, xenophobia, classism, ageism etc.) are all interconnected and cannot be seen, challenged or unravelled separately. This concept first came from Kimberlé Crenshaw in 1989, and helps us to understand the complexities of individual experience and systemic oppressions.

Feminisms?
For as many women as there are in the world, there are arguably as many feminisms. Check them out sometime! Eco-feminism, Marxist, socialist, mana wahine, radical, liberal, post-modern, post-structural, anarcha-fem, new age, black, womanist, separatist, cultural, lesbian, Chicana, standpoint, libertarian... feminism to name a few.

Heteronormativity
Heteronormativity is the action of a gender essentialist's ideal world, one in which men and women fall into distinct categories with clear roles and expectations, where heterosexuality is the norm reinforced in power structures such as legislation and the media.

Heterosexism
Attitudes, bias and discriminations that favour opposite sex relationships and heteronormativity. It is based on the presumption that people are heterosexual – the expected 'superior' norm.

Heteropatriarchy
The powerful combination of a heterosexually biased society run by a patriarchy. Most nation-states and ruling classes could be described as such. From America to Saudi Arabia, from New Zealand to Indonesia. Where straight men rule the roost.

Homosocialisation
Where people socialise with their own gender most of the time, or in certain situations such as work or sports teams. Homosocialisation reinforces gender stereotypes, gender roles, gendered division of time, education and work. It is self-perpetuating.

TERF
An acronym for Trans-Exclusionary Radical Feminist. Feminists who state that trans-women aren't really women, thinking the only women are those born with a vagina and XX chromosomes. Gender essentialists through and through.

SWERF
Sex Worker Exclusionary Radical Feminism, which opposes women's participation in prostitution and pornography. Their ideology and that of TERFs, follow a prescriptive, heteronormative approach to feminism.

An internet troll/trolling
Someone who finds pleasure in seeking opportunities to disrupt and derail discussions and debates in online forums, blogs and social media. For the fun of pointless argument, and sometimes more sinisterly, to meaninglessly detract attention from important conversations.

Male gaze
When the audience is constructed from the assumed perspective of heterosexual men. The male gaze is so powerful in media that it now dictates the content of most mainstream films, TV, music videos and advertisements. Men are situated as the watchers, women as watched; men active, women passive. Buy the product, get the girl or be the girl. Think car ads, female roles in action films, main characters on TV and superheroes.

Rape culture
Rape culture as a term is designed to show the ways in which society blames victims of sexual assault and normalises male sexual violence. It is a culture that encourages boys and men to be macho and aggressive, and girls and women to be submissive and compliant. A society that allows a quarter of women and girls to be raped or sexually assaulted, and 1/6 of men and boys. Where 3 per cent of rapists are jailed after just 6 per cent of rapes and assaults are ever reported. A social culture in which rape jokes and cat calls are heard and normalised, where the male gaze pervades pop music and the visual arts. Where children are sexualised by clothing and toy companies. Rape culture has implications for all and is everyone's issue regardless of gender.

Filament *series* >>
Brie Sherow

I've noticed that women are often reluctant to take part in conversations when they're unsure of the answers. I think that it's important to remember that no-one definitively has the answers, but we can come closer to some meaningful truths when everyone participates equally in the conversation. I use collage as a way to explore new concepts. These are mixed media pieces that combine my film photography, images found in magazines, and discarded filament from 3D printers.

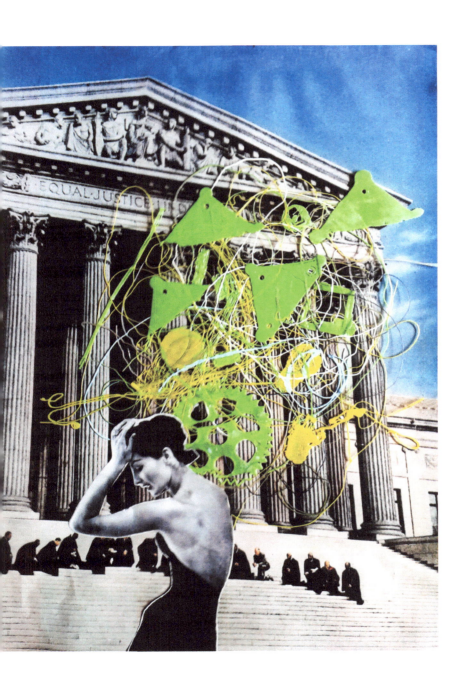

62 FEMINISM AND TECHNOLOGY WOR(L)DS

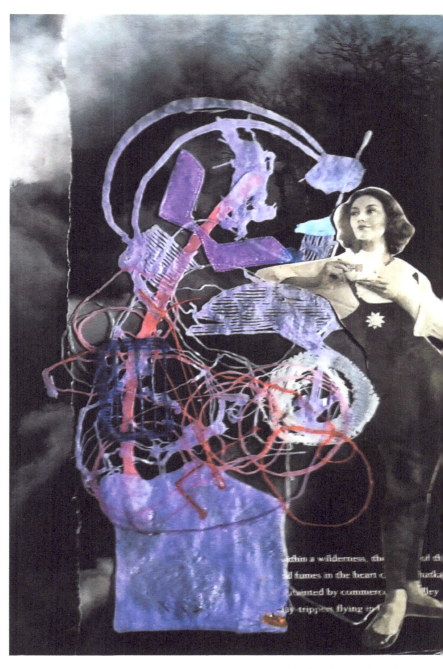

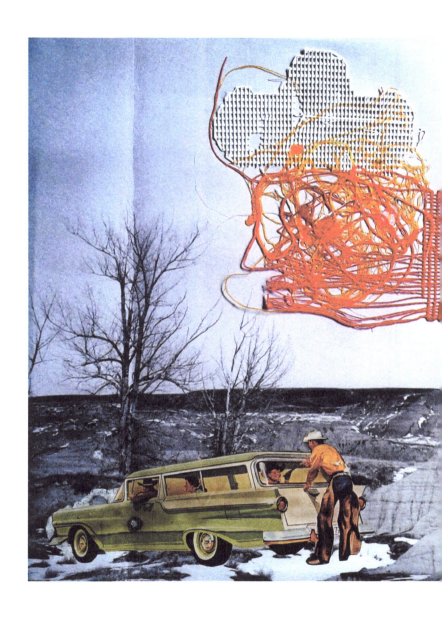

FILAMENT SERIES 67

Freeranger
of the issue

\>\>

Sheila Kitzinger

FREERANGER OF THE ISSUE 69

> There are many women who hope for child-birth in which they, not the doctors, are in control. They want to have the information that will enable them to make their own decisions, to prepare themselves for an experience in which they participate fully, and do not wish labour and birth to be taken over by managers…This may be either in their own home, or in a birth centre in which the rhythms of a labouring woman's body are honoured and waited on, and where birth in non-interventionist and centred on people instead of mechianical proccesses.
>
> Sheila Kitzinger, *Homebirth: The Essential Guide to Giving Birth Outside of The Hospital*

Sheila Kitzinger was a British anthropologist, natural birth activist and author. She died in Oxfordshire aged 86 years on 11 April 2015. She was a remarkable women – an early second wave feminist who advocated for the underrepresented and provided women with the information they needed in order to have their own knowledge and voices. She did this by educating women about the physiology of pregnancy, birth and breastfeeding; the process of birth; what technological interventions were available and the risks they entailed. She understood the power of technology in birth and of those who used it, as well as the innate power women hold in birthing their babies.

As a child in the 1930s, Sheila would hide behind the couch, listening to her mother dispence advice and information to women (and sometimes men) in her role as a organiser of an early family planning group. These listening sessions shaped Sheila's world. From an early age, she saw sexuality, pregnancy and birth as integral to the lives of women and their families. She had always felt there was nothing mysterious or shameful in thinking about, planning for and discussing these parts of our lives. She studied anthropology at university and went on to explore the pregnancy, birthing and childcare practices in regions as diverse as the Carribean, North and South America (including indigenous peoples), Africa and Europe as well as countries such as China and Australia. From this research she formed the view that it was women who needed to dictate the terms of the births, that it was women who knew best (when they were sufficiently educated) and needed to be supported in their own strength and confidence in birthing.

During the 1950s, at the height of the medicalisation of childbirth, Sheila believed women in most countries were not supported as such. All around her she saw traumatised and disempowered women, suffering from unnecessary intervention and loss of knowledge and control in birth. She set out to change this. In 1956 she and her husband Uwe decided on a homebirth for their first daughter (the first of five). This was deemed highly outrageous and dangerous. However Sheila was firm in her belief that all women who have non–high risk pregnancies should be encouraged or at least be able to choose whether they birth at home, in a birthing centre or a hospital. She believed that their pregnancies and births should be treated physiologically, not pathologically, and that they should be fully educated about all aspects of pregnancy and birth, including the potential effects of intervention, in order to exercise true choice.

Until WWII homebirth was standard in Britain and much of the Western world, and despite ongoing medicalisation of childbirth, remains standard in the majority of the world today, but no longer in the West. In her research Sheila observed the great need for technological intervention in births where mother or baby were at risk of disease or death – and how maternal and infant deaths had plummeted dramatically due to these advances in knowledge. However, she saw an increasing shift away from a women-centred approach to a 'healthy mother, healthly baby – at all costs' approach – where babies are birthed by passive mothers using interventions ranging from other people's hands to technology, which disregards natural instincts, possible subsequent effects (cascade of intervention), ongoing trauma and post-birth issues such as problems breastfeeding and bonding. She questioned what 'healthy' meant in this instance and demanded that the mental health of mothers and babies be included in this definition. She believed that the scales had tipped from the point where babies and mothers were greatly benefiting from technology in birth to its over zealous use, where hospitals and doctors treated women like patients who were 'done to', rather than as active birthers, to be supported as they wished.

As a strident feminist, Sheila was taken aback when attacked publicly for her 'anti-feminist' ideology by women she had known and worked with. These liberal feminists felt strongly that she was advocating robbing women of their choice to a pain-free childbirth, also claiming she was prolonging women's unnessesary suffering. In response Sheila promoted the term 'pain with purpose'. She famously said 'Birth isn't something we suffer but something we do actively and exult in!'(Freedom for Birth). For without pain, she knew women could not feel what was happening in their bodies during labour and therefore not know what to do and when, as well as being able to differentiate between normal pain, and pain where something is going wrong.

Sheila responded to such criticisims of her work by stating that she never meant to vilify individual women for how their births play out, but that the medicial and social structures that saw women's reproductive processes controlled largely by men and technology needed to be changed. She gave extreme examples of female prisoners in many countries (and still in some US states today) birthing babies in chains, stripped of power, choice and dignity, and attended to mainly by male doctors and guards. She has been instrumental in drawing attention to such abuses of power and the degradation of women, and in ending such practices.

Defence of her work continued with further examples of women who were given the option of pain relief at the height of their most painful contractions, women who had no prior knowledge of the benefits and risks of the drugs. Drugs no longer routinely used, such as pethidine, make women drowsy and less able to push their babies out. They can interfere with the baby's breathing and breast feeding suck for several days after birth. Sheila asked, how do these risks compare to a relatively short lived pain, which women are able to manage? It imnfuriated her that women were infantilised by having information withheld from them on the assumption that they could not understand technology and their own bodies.

Sheila is the author of more than thirty books and was made an Honourary Professor at the University of West London. She completed her autobiography A Passion For Birth shortly before for her death and worked for a birth crisis network in England and campaigned for the rights of women the world over. She encouraged women to reclaim their bodies, reclaim their power and delight in the births of their babies, however they saw fit.

In achieving the depersonalization of childbirth and at the same time solving the problem of pain, our society may have lost more than it has gained. We are left with the physical husk; the transcending significance has been drained away.

Women as Mothers, 1978.

Works cited

www.sheilakitzinger.com

Kitzinger, Shelia. "Freedom for Birth." Film. Web, 19 May 2015. http://www.freedomforbirth.com.

Kitzinger, Sheila. *Homebirth: The Essential Guide to Giving Birth Outside of The Hospital.* Dorling Kindersley, 1991.

Kitzinger, Shelia. *Passion for Birth: My Life: Anthropology, Family and Feminism.* London: Pinter and Martin, 2015.

Kitzinger, Shelia. *Women as Mothers.* London: Random House, 1978.

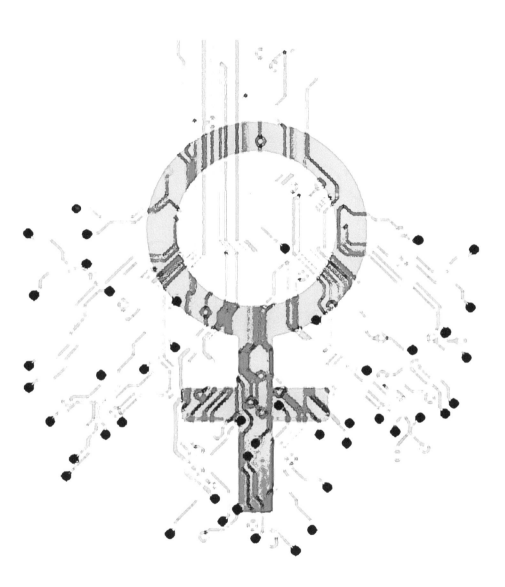

Hey Girl:
The faces and voices of the new online fourth wave feminism

\>\>

Paula Van Beek

Now that there is a Feminist Ryan Gosling 'Hey Girl' meme, we know that social media and online spaces are playing a key role in giving greater visibility and voice to feminist issues. As reported in *The Telegraph* by Radhika Sanghani, two Canadian PhD students have proved a link between viewing Gosling's handsome face overlaid with academic feminist texts and the endorsement of feminist beliefs. In surveying recent posts, tweets and campaigns we can see that online activity is in fact creating and shaping an emerging fourth wave feminism.

The suffragettes worked hard for gender equality giving women the vote and second–wave feminists fought for liberation across sexuality, reproductive rights and the workplace. If the claim of third wave feminism (which arose around the 1990s) is true – that we can now allow women to incorporate their own identities into the belief system of what feminism is and what it can become – then is the WomenAgainstFeminism Facebook page with its 30,561 likes, actually anti-feminist at all? WomenAgainstFeminism images first appeared on Tumblr in July 2013. These sites display selfies with signs – women expressing their own individual understanding of feminism and equality. Whether they may make you groan or grin they have sparked reactions right across the interweb. Right now the F-word is getting a lot of screen time.

The internet is facilitating an emerging fourth wave feminism. Stepping away from its third wave white middle-class roots, this new wave seeks to mobilise everyone of any race, educational background, gender or LGBTI identification. Graffiti, zines, and T-shirt slogans are now replaced with witty blog posts, Facebook pages, memes and tweets as cyperspace becomes the place to call out male privilege and clarify the concerns of feminism.

#WhyINeedFeminism is an earnest response to the WomenAgainstFeminism movement. Spread across Youtube, Tumblr, Facebook and Twitter #WhyINeedFeminism gives women a space to share their experiences of everyday double standards and assert that the work of feminism is not finished. But a more direct response, with Twitter tongue firmly in cheek, is @NoToFeminism with its tagline 'lol feminsim no thanks'.

Taking the in-jokes one step further, and many are saying one step too far, are pro-misandrist sites such as the Male-Tears Tumblr. Yip, they are playing with the accusation (with a large dose of irony) that the empowerment of women leads to the oppression of men. They rejoice in bathing in the male tears of men's rights' activists who cry of sexism against men. They're making a joke from the misguided notion that feminists are man-haters. They are also making T-shirts and novelty mugs.

It just wouldn't be the internet without a whole lot of cats. David Futrelle, cat lover and Confused Cats Against

Feminism Tumblr instigator, is savvy to this. Cat selfies with signs that confuse feminism with tuna ('I don't need it if I can't eat it') are mocking the WomenAgainstFeminism sites. These confused cats and Male-Tears T-shirts are taking anti-feminist ideas right through to their illogical conclusions to show that they are ridiculous. In exaggerating and criticising anti-feminist stances they avoid having to wade into the successes and failures of feminism itself, allowing room for the emergence of fourth-wave inclusiveness. Humour proves to be a useful strategy to keep the conversation about feminism evolving.

Taking the F-word to the masses is the United Nations #HeForShe campaign. Emma Watson (famous for her portrayal of the head-strong Hermoine in some movies about a wizard) is the face and voice of this campaign. She offered an invitation to men to join in the gender

equality movement. The YouTube upload of the heartfelt campaign speech went viral with over three million views in three days after its September 2014 launch. '… fighting for women's rights has too often become synonymous with man-hating,' Watson said. 'For the record, feminism by definition is the belief that men and women should have equal rights and opportunities.' She seemed to be speaking directly to the 'I don't need feminism' signs and to the misandrist movement too. Within only a few days 126,000 boys and men had pledged their support to the campaign.

The #HeforShe campaign has been questioned by articulate detractors debating the validity of putting men's experience at the centre of the feminist cause – but more sinisterly Emma Watson herself has been attacked in an online intimidation campaign. As soon as the UN standing ovation was over the trolling

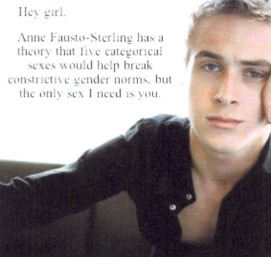

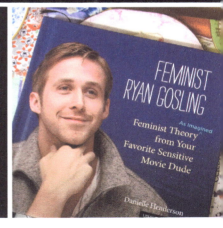

HEY GIRL 77

began. There were fake reports of her death, and the website emmayouarenext.com appeared, staging a countdown to when nude photographs of the young celebrity would be 'leaked'. The focus was being turned from a young woman's voice to her body. This is not a new tactic.

Social media users contributing to pro-feminist campaigns, such as #YesAllWomen and #WhyINeedFeminism, are often victims of vile personal attacks on their physical appearance and femininity (or perceived lack thereof). This is a way of steering the conversation away from the real issues and focusing on image instead. It would seem that, even in 2015, women who think and talk are seen as a threat. Beauty is one of the few forms of currency women are allowed. However it is a slippery commodity. In championing achievements and opinions over image, some 'ugly' feminists are happy to devalue their beauty dollar in order to be heard.

As a tactic to take the power of appearances back, Twitter user LilyBolourian tweeted a selfie in July 2014 with the satirical hashtag #FeministsAreUgly. She encouraged others to share their 'ugly' feminist faces: 'For women, particularly of color, owning our appearance is a radical act.' Within a month the hashtag was tweeted out over 91,000 times. Also owning the insult is The Royal Holloway University of London Feminist Club that started the #UglyGirlsClub after an insult was overheard about their committee members. Their Facebook 'ugly selfie' campaign had over 4500 likes within less than a month of launching in November 2014 with many other universities joining the cause.

Anita Sarkeesian, pop culture commentator and creator of the Feminist Frequency website, asserts that cyberbullying and hate campaigns are widespread strategies

Sometimes I look cracking and sometimes I say stuff that's cracking. The stuff I say lasts longer. #uglygirlsclub

I took a special picture for all the misogynist whiners in my feed today. #bestvacationever

to maintain the internet as a male dominated space, an online boys club. The emmayouarenext.com countdown was in fact a hoax by a gang of internet pranksters. Even though it was a false threat the concern is that the culture of online harassment of women is so prevalent that publishing unauthorised nude photos was seen a perfectly plausible response to a young women asserting feminist views. In hindsight the countdown highlighted that no one was asking why – only waiting for when. But the increased media coverage proved that any publicity can be good publicity – there was a huge response supporting the #HeForShe campaign. This demonstrates a small cultural shift towards achieving gender equality on and off line. Nevertheless women remain the most visible and vulnerable within the web.

It's easy to get trapped in an echo chamber on the internet where you're only seeking out and receiving information that already fits your feminist worldview. The WomenAgainstFeminism sites were certainly a shock – yet the increased visibility of (pro or anti) feminist images is actively encouraging a wider engagement in questioning and defining what feminism can mean to all people. Responsiveness, evolution and revolution seem to be built into the very fabric of feminism. The emerging fourth-wave, enabled by social media as the predominant media platform, is creating space for multiple voices and faces to respond to issues of patriarchy and privilege.

And there is always room on the internet for Ryan Gosling and some cute looking cats.

I DON'T NEED FEMINISM BECAUSE...

• FEM DOESN'T MEAN EQUALITY
• THE PAY GAP IS WOMENS CHOICE, NOT SEXISM
• THE PATRIARCHY DOESN'T EXIST
• MOST VICTIMS OF STREET VIOLENCE ARE MEN
• I'M RESPONSIBLE FOR MY OWN ACTIONS
• THERE IS NO RAPE CULTURE

I don't need feminism because it defiles my dream to become a boy loving stay at home wife. I also don't need feminism because it destroys fam...

Works cited

Sanghani, Radhika. 'Feminist Ryan Gosling memes are changing men's minds.' *The Telegraph* 02 Feb. 2015. Web.

HerForShe, Emma Watson HeForShe Speech at the United Nations.' Online video clip. *YouTube*. YouTube, 22 Sept. 2014. Web. 24 Sept. 2014.

Bolourian, Lily, (LilyBolourian) "For women, particularly of color, owning our appearance is a radical act.' 7 Aug 2014, 11:46 am. Tweet.

WomanAgainstFeminism @NoToFeminism · Aug 24
I don't need fisimes because women like Beyoncé are fismests and NOBODY likes her everybody hates her

1.2K   1.4K

the endle
Only 2 ho
Reply

80   FEMINISM AND TECHNOLOGY WOR(L)DS

For your viewing pleasure:

feministryangosling.tumblr.com
womenagainstfeminism.tumblr.com
twitter.com/notofeminism
confusedcatsagainstfeminism.tumblr.com
wehuntedthemammoth.com

male-tears.tumblr.com
heforshe.org
www.emmayouarenext.com
facebook.com/selfiecampaign
feministfrequency.com

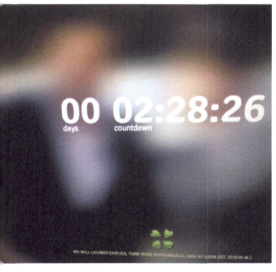

WomanAgainstFeminism @NoToFeminism · Oct 19

I don't need feimsins even the weather is misandrist!!!!!!!!

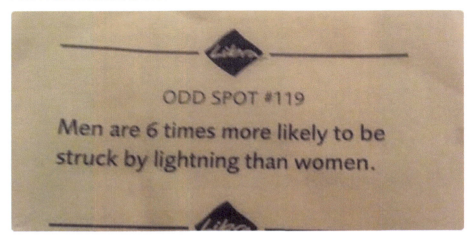

#whyineedfeminism thanks patriarchy for creating stereotypes like this around movements for equality

 Cuz I can't tweet/say my opinion without trolls trying to argue against it. #whyineedfeminism

 Because today my school had a meeting about dress code, but only for girls #everydaysexism #whyineedfeminism @femfreq @EverydaySexism

 R @RyanGabatino · 5h
#HerForShe I never expected waking up today as a feminist.

 Simon Pegg ✓
@simonpegg   ✩ ⋯ Follow

Husband to a wife, father to a daughter, son to a mother. You bet I'm on board, @EmWatson! #heforshe

HEY GIRL 83

Cheap'n'Choice: *the Wikibomb*

\>\>

Byron Kinnaird

'Wikipedia needs women editors. Badly.' Freelance writer and retired programmer and analyst Dawn Leonard Tripp is not exaggerating – research suggests Wikipedia's editorial body is 85-90 per cent male. 'The dearth of women's voices on Wikipedia,' she continues, 'means that its readers are informed by a colossal, electronic Cyclops. To be fair, much of the gender bias on Wikipedia is probably unconscious and not the result of an army of misogynists plotting to set civilization back 100 years.' Even so, this cyclopic army of editors need some balance, which is where the Wikibomb comes in.

Wiki-editing groups such as the WikiWomen's Collaborative and Architexx, which systematically diversify Wikipedia's monocular gender bias are collectively awarded this issue's Cheap'n'Choice Award, for sending forth their Wikibombs in the fight against gender bias and underrepresentation of women online.

For example, aspiring architects around the world can now find out about Rachel Nolan, Alexis Ord and Sandra Kaji-O'Grady thanks to a global initiative Women. Wikipedia. Design. (#WikiD) led by Architexx, to increase the representation of notable female architects on Wikipedia. Founded by Nina Freedman and Lori Brown, Architexx (www. architexx.org) realised it was time for action this year, and sought to inaugurate an annual global effort 'to have the most diverse and wide ranging of women written in ... because there are so many women to write about.' Australian-based advocacy community, Parlour (archiparlour.org) picked up the call and mobilised wikiparties across the country, tripling the number of Australians on the List of Women Architects. Depressingly, New Zealand currently has only one entry on this list, Kate Beath, 'probably the first (and apparently only) female architect in New Zealand.'

As Despina Stratigakos put it in her powerful and must-read article "Unforgetting Women Architects: From the Pritzker to Wikipedia": 'History is not a simple meritocracy: it is a narrative of the past written and revised — or not written at all — by people with agendas.' She invites us to 'intervene to ensure the presence of women architects in online histories — which is increasingly important to do as the web becomes a primary site for making and preserving the cultural record.'

Dawn Leonard Tripp's online article 'How to Edit Wikipedia: Lessons from a Female Contributor' is an excellent instructional starting point if you're not sure how to get started on Wikipedia. You can also find support by joining the WikiWomen's Collaborative on facebook or on twitter (@WikiWomen).

ARCHITEXX
WE ASK HOW NOT IF

WOMEN. WIKIPEDIA. DESIGN

MARCH 8 2015

SIGN UP:

wikiD

This spread and previous page: Architexx WikiD event held at the Centre for Architecture, New York, in 2015.

Beyoncé, Björk & Beats

>> *Jessie Moss*

Melody Thomas, Radio New Zealand broadcaster and journalist, met with producer and singer Estère Dalton and myself, a songwriter, writer and feminist, on a sunny, still autumn morning. As we converged in a Newtown kitchen from different corners of Wellington city, conversation quickly turned to the music industry.

Melody recounts an article about Björk we've both recently read, detailing Björk's constant battle to be recognised as the producer of her own music in the male-dominated industry. One question that she is commonly confronted with – 'Who produces your music?' – instantly reinforces gender stereotypes and downplays her abilities. Estère understands – she deals with the same assumptions about her music.

We move on to Beyoncé, and how differently women can function in the music industry, whether they are self-produced or managed by the machine.
'Is Beyoncé really a feminist?'
'Her beliefs aren't always evident in her lyrics, videos, dance moves and outfits though'
'But Björk is outlandish and sings about sex too'.
'It's about who says what, and the context though…'
'Stop for a minute, we've got to record this', I say. We move rooms and hit record.

Jessie - What does feminism mean to you and what place does it have in your life?

Estère – To me it means equality of opportunity and respect.

L-R Melody Thomas, Jessie Moss and Estère Dalton

Melody – It's exactly the same for me. In my life, that practice is mostly to do with my daughter, raising her so that she is aware of those things.

J to M – What place do you see feminism holding in your professional life as a broadcaster and journalist?

M – Having a feminist base gives me a lot of courage when asking for what I want, not holding back and believing that I can do those things. Within the organisation at Radio New Zealand there are a few really inspiring women, and I get a real buzz knowing these women are there if I need them, to reach out and ask advice.

J – Do you think there are just as many female as male presenters and journalists on air?

M – It depends where you are looking in the organisation. Within the presenters I'd say women are quite well represented, which is fantastic. I'm not sure if Radio New Zealand makes a point of this but I wouldn't be surprised. But if you look at the engineers the majority are male and it's the same when you look at the top tier – the heads of departments. It is very much a boys club at that level.

It is very much a boys club at that level.

J – Research shows all the areas that wrap around music, broadcasting, media and publicity are horizontally and vertically segregated. Vertically you will see the powerful structures at the top dominated by men, down to the cleaners of organisations who are most likely to be women. Horizontally men and women congregate together in gendered areas, such as women more often being publicists – the pretty voice and face of organisations.

M – That's interesting because one of the first things we were taught from the beginning at broadcasting school, when we are learning how to speak on radio, is that people find women's vocal frequencies agitating to the ear – we are taught to lower our voices!

E – In respected news media, there is a common tendency with presenters for an equal ratio of men and women. I don't know about behind the scenes.

M – Television is different though isn't it, because all those women are really good

BEYONCÉ, BJÖRK & BEATS

looking, a nice conventionally attractive face, nothing too abrasive so you just soak up what they are saying.

E – You could say that about the men too, except for the older guys.

M – I think men can get away with a bit more. I remember reading about a male news presenter last year, who wore the same cheap suit everyday as a test, because his female partner got letters daily about what she was wearing, mostly being criticised. It was a year before anyone noticed.

J – Estère, do you see feminism playing out in you life?

E – Definitely when it comes to being represented as a musician or producer as opposed to just a singer. That is something that I am very aware of and put a lot of emphasis on, or else I feel it will get washed away (being a producer). There are just so many more men sitting in their bedrooms, making music.

M – We have a friend staying from England, and I showed him your video last night, he said it was so cool to see girls play instruments.

E – It is so cool!

M – Yeah, but I wish it wasn't like that, 'Wow look at that woman playing the guitar'.

E – Like seeing Sheep Dog Wolf play yesterday, and the female bass player, I couldn't take my eyes off her.

M – And a girl on a horn as well . . . fuck, I wish it wasn't like that.

E – And there are gendered instruments – you're more likely to see a girl on horn instruments. I would say that saxophone is middle ground.

M – But moody female bassists are a thing! Smashing Pumpkins' D'Arcy!

J – When people talk about women playing instruments, it's mentioned: 'the female drummer' and so on. On the one hand it's good to draw attention to women playing, but should it even have to be mentioned?

M – It would be nice if we lived in a world where it didn't have to be mentioned. But for the 10-year-old girl, I think it should be said.

E – Yes it needs to be emphasised. It would lead to more active movement towards the end goal if it is talked about and highlighted.

J – If you are in a band of female players, a 'girl band', and labelled as such, how would you feel Estère?

My question is how do men get to that position where they are sitting in the engineer's studio producing music for other people?

E – It depends on the capacity. If it was just a girl band because of having only women in it, then that is stupid – guys wouldn't get that label. Only if there are five singers out the front, like with boy bands. Only if it is equal.

M – It's interesting though, because it's a great marketing tool, like you were saying in your TED talk that while the female musician thing really grates you, it's also given you opportunities, a selling point, people want you in their magazine.
J – What do you say to the rise of home recording, and demystification of the recording process, meaning that women now have greater access to creating music without having to rely on boys clubs in studios? Could this be interpreted as being 're-segregated' into a lower status of music production rather than being assimilated into the recording industry?

E – The world is much more open and easier to explore, so I don't think the home studio is any less…

M – It seems out dated eh? But at the start, people wanted to keep hold of the power in the studio.

E – My question is how do men get to that position where they are sitting in the engineer's studio producing music for other people? Because I want to do that! I think that studio production is seen as a more polished way of doing it, but it's becoming more and more redundant.

M – With his last Unknown Mortal Orchestra album I'm pretty sure Ruban Nielson recorded most of his vocals at home into a dictaphone and Flying Lotus does it all in his home. With heaps of a flash gear.

E – But there are no female producers with his (Flying Lotus) status at that level. There are definitely more male beatmakers and producers out there. I think this is due to a lack of role models – women don't really associate themselves as much with the beats/producer culture in comparison to their male counterparts. That being said, there are still some girls out there representing.

J –What is your experience of collaborating with others, finding people to work with?

M – I'm lucky with Music 101, we are mostly women. But interestingly, I sometimes feel very much like I am the only one looking out for myself, like

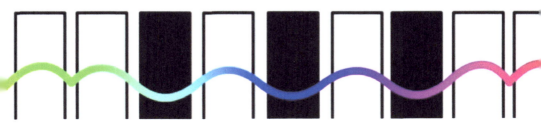

there is this unnecessary competition. And I'm guilty of it! Another producer came on-board recently and I caught myself diminishing her and her work, and actively had to stop myself. It's almost as if you feel like there are only so many places for women in the industry and you don't want to give yours up. What a sad state of affairs that is! I'd be curious to know if men feel like they have to protect their place.

E – Good point, I'd say the same for me.

M – I'm meeting with Carol Hirschfeld tomorrow, who's the new Head of Content for RNZ, and it might be unrealistic but now I have this feeling that there is someone at the top who will see that there are amazing women at RNZ and who will help get them to where they want to go. And it's ridiculous for me to expect that just because she is a female in a high position that she now has to champion us.

J to E – If there are three bands in a gig, and only one woman in the mix, she will stick out more, and get more relative criticism. Do you feel you have to work harder to get to where you are, because you are so visible as a beatmaker?

M – You have a surprise element though and because it's not a traditional instrument there is less expectation around it, and how well you might play it.

E – People are surprised by my beats, impressed by the beats. I really like making beats and I'm confident. I have very clear musical vision and I don't really care what anyone else thinks in terms of that capacity. You need to hold on to that, you can be affected by things about musicianship, being a female. When I hang around with heaps of boys that went to jazz school, cause I don't know any theory, I just retain my faith in my own musical abilities. I know what I like. I'm not going to let insecurity compromise that.

M – I am going to start working with a new presenter soon, a man who has years of experience, and I feel like I'm in way over my head but I'm just going ahead with it anyway hoping that I'll pass the test.

E – I don't think that guys feel like this too, none of this 'I don't know what I am going to do, or doing'.

J – Do you think that women are more uncertain . . . second-guess themselves?

E – It's constructed that they would. Not only is it a reality they are given far fewer role models and are less encouraged, girls and boys are brought up in gender constructs, like going out and playing trucks and climbing trees. Females are encouraged to be analytical. I don't think that same culture exists around men. Stopping themselves and starting again.

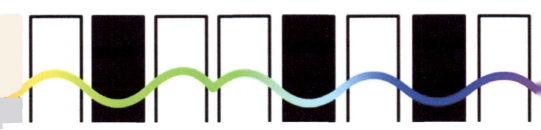

M – I've read somewhere that women are less likely to do something they don't think they'll succeed at, to even try.

J – What were you both interested in and encouraged to do as children?

M – A big part of my confidence comes from growing up on a farm with a really ungendered upbringing. I don't even remember feeling like a girl as a child. Jumping in rivers and rescuing lambs!

E – Open to explore things.

M – I was interested in writing and music but they both disappeared as interests when my parents split when I was eleven. For a while anyway. But my parents raised me so well, the only criticism I have is they pushed me to get a degree to 'fall back on'. We were told we could do whatever we want, as long as we worked hard enough at it.

E – I liked to read and to make things, like sculptures out of old flower stems. I liked singing.

And with visions of Estère and Melody as lamb-rescuing, countryside-wandering flower sculptors, our interesting conversation abruptly comes to an end. My baby has woken from her nap. Her cries and our coos intermingle on my Garageband interview as chatter turns from the music industry to a cute baby.

> *I have very clear musical vision and I don't really care what anyone else thinks in terms of that capacity.*

Further viewing

Adventure Artists. "I Spy by Estère". Online video clip. *YouTube*, 6 Apr. 2014. Web. <www.youtube.com/watch?v=3KVjT5d0OUc>

TEDXTalks. "Girls in the beat world: Estere at TEDxVUW". Online video clip. *Youtube*, 24 Apr. 2014. Web. <www.youtube.com/watch?v=wOC8dKgM_5U>

Contributors

\>\>

Jessie Moss – editor
Jessie grew up along the banks of the Avon river in Christchurch with the Moss' and Lockes and now resides in Newtown, Wellington, with her young family. As a feminist she seeks opportunities to speak truth to power, holding our patriarchal-capitalist societies to account. As a mother she works hard to create strong resilient communities where raising children is everyone's business. She is also a teacher, committed to inclusive education practices, where teaching and learning is reciprocal and equitable for all, for the common good.

Maia McDonald – designer
Maia Robin McDonald is a Buddhist, ceramic artist, photographer, poet and graphic designer, from Taranaki, New Zealand. She is currently practicing as a designer and will soon be completing a Ceramics project for enjoy Art Gallery (to be installed in September 2015).
Ceramics: www.okouku.co.nz

Susanna Fiore
Susanna is a British-Italian actor, singer and theatre-maker based in London. She co-founded the critically acclaimed theatre company The Ruby Dolls six years ago. She has training in 'Theatre in Prisons and Probation' and has designed and facilitated creative workshops for several high-security UK prisons, and for N.E.E.T (Not in Education, Employment or Training) teenagers in London. She is interested in theatre created for non-theatre spaces and is currently writing her first independent, full-length play.
www.therubydolls.com

Mani Bruce Mitchell
Taupo-nui-a-tia College, Dip ED, Dip T. Waikato University.
Out intersex queer identified, gender fluid, international: Change Agent, Counsellor, Artist, Clinical Supervisor, Media consultant, Educator, Lecturer and Executive Director of ITANZ (Intersex Trust Aotearoa NZ). Mani is involved in the making of numerous films and documentaries about intersex and gender variance, including the internationally successful film Intersexion.

Melissa Chambers
Now working in New York and London, Melissa is an Australian Theatre Director who holds a BA in Dramatic Arts from the Victorian College of the Arts in Melbourne. She is currently completing a Masters degree at the Royal Central School of Speech and Drama, London. In 2014 she was an artist in residence at The Freight in New York where she began developing a performance based on the life and work of Ada Byron. Melissa was raised in Brisbane by an Art Historian and a Software Engineer. She is interested in getting better at maths.
www.mchambers.com

Rosie Downing
As midwife and nurse Rosie has a long standing interest in social health, and a special desire to expose and remediate the impacts of colonialism and racism. She now lives, works and wanders around the central Australian desert. She has made her own zines, one about maps and one about letters, and this is her first contribution to Freerange Press.

Huia Welton
Huia describes herself as a raging leftie, feminist, mama and dyke. She lives in Te Whanganui-a-Tara, Wellington, and loves that city with its wind and stormy seas.

Marianne Bevan
Marianne has worked for non-governmental organisations in West Africa and Government Ministries in Aotearoa-New Zealand. Her work and academic research has tended to focus on the gendered experiences of conflict, crime and policing. She currently lives in Wellington, Aotearoa New Zealand and is helping to set up a book club for women in prison.

Felicity Scarce
Based in Brisbane, Australia, Felicity writes and creates visual art. Her practices explore constructions of contemporary spirituality that we cannot quite name – everyday magic and the rituals we create for ourselves. Her favourite routines include swimming in the ocean and looking in the letterbox.

Brie Sherow
Brie is a mixed media collage artist who combines her own photography and creations with magazine clippings and found objects. In the *Filament Series*, she uses the waste from 3D printers to add another dimension to her collages. More of her work can be found at *http://messamerica.tumblr.com*.

Paula van Beek
Paula is an artist dedicated to making and supporting contemporary image-driven performance projects. Her work investigates self, identity, locality and alternative narrative structures with a focus on feminine experiences. She is currently undertaking a Research Masters at RMIT School of Fine Art, Melbourne.
www.paulavanbeek.com

Byron Kinnaird
Byron is a New Zealand-born teacher, researcher and creative practitioner based in Melbourne. He is completing at PhD in Architecture titled 'Negotiating Educations' at the University of Melbourne, and is producing a series of works on Australian fire.
www.drawnandwritten.com

Estère Dalton
Estère is a girl with an MPC she calls Lola. With Lola, Estère samples and records a wide variety of sounds, which she uses to create a canvas of pulsating rhythms and evocative melodies. Her elastic voice and inquisitive lyrics help paint Estère's own unique genre of 'Electric Blue Witch-Hop'.

Melody Thomas
Melody Thomas is a national broadcaster, columnist and mother who lives in Island Bay, Wellington. She was expelled from Wellington Girls' High School for throwing a tennis ball at the principal's head in assembly, and would go on to be made 'Dux' in her final year at Aotea College. She is currently co-producing music review show The Sampler with Nick Bollinger.
radionz.co.nz/national/programmes/thesampler
radionz.co.nz/music101

Image credits

Apart from individual listings, images throughout by or supplied by Maia McDonald.

Page 18
Image courtesy of Mani Mitchell and ILGA 'International lesbian, gay, tran and intersex association ilga.org

Page 27
Ada Byron by William Henry Mote

Page 28
Image by Tom and Katrien, Creative Commons licence CC BY SA 2.0

Pages 32-33
Photo by Tawhai Moss, courtesy of Jessie Moss and Mara TK

Pages 36-37
Two mums imagery sourced by Maia from www.graphicstock.com

Pages 40-43
Images courtesy of Glenna Gordon

Pages 54 & 57
Gender symbols by Caaloba sourced from deviantart.com.

Page 69
Shelia Kitzinger Image courtesy of Boston Association for Childbirth Education

Page 76-83
All images discovered by Paula Van Beek as listed below

01 Confused cat
confusedcatsagainstfeminism.tumblr.com

02 Ryan Gosling
feministryangosling.tumblr.com
Hey Girl Book
feministryangosling.tumblr.com

03 Ulgydirlsclub
facebook.com/selfiecampaign

04 Feminists Are Ugly
https://twitter.com/hashtag/FeministsAreUgly

06 Women against Feminism x 2
womenagainstfeminism.tumblr.com

07 No To Feminism Beyonce
https://twitter.com/notofeminism

08
Emma Watson fake death.jpg
emmayouarenext
www.emmayouarenext.com (now re-directing to RANTIC site)

09 i bathe in male tears tshirt

09 mug
http://male-tears.tumblr.com/

09 T-shirt tweet
https://twitter.com/jessicavalenti/status/494591618519805953

10 HeForShe

10 waking up a feminist
https://twitter.com/heforshe

Pages 84-87
Images courtesy of Sarah Rafson and Lori Brown.

Page 89
Photo by Tawhai Moss

Recent books published by Freerange Press

Christchurch: The Transitional City Pt IV
Once in a Lifetime: City-building after Disaster in Christchurch

Journals

Freerange Vol. 1: The Self and the City
Freerange Vol. 2. Gardening and Violence
Freerange Vol. 3: The Trickster
Freerange Vol. 4: Almost Home
Freerange Vol. 5: Dangerous and Wrong
Freerange Vol. 6: The Untitled Issue
Freerange Vol. 7: The Commons
Freerange Vol. 8: Humanimal 3.0
Freerange Vol. 9: The Wet Issue

Other books published

Analogue Architecture: Between Imagination and Memory
Chur Chur: Stories from the Christchurch Earthquake
Congress Book V1.0
Crowd-share Innovation: Intensive, creative collaborations
Infostructures: A Transport and Research Project
Practicing: U.Lab Handbook of Design
Tsuanmi Box
Youtopia: A Passion for the Dark